Came With All Power

Vol 4

Holly Vaughan

Copyright, 2025 Holly Vaughan

Measurement

Shaping Things

And the porch before the temple of the house, twenty cubits was the length thereof, according to the breadth of the house; and ten cubits was the breadth thereof before the house.

1 Kings 6:3

Before we get any further, here's a quick look at what exactly is meant by all this building going on in the picture. Here's the length, width, and height explained in sum by what had been meant from the start. If you remember, the formula for area was

$$length \times width$$

Where x stand for times or multiplied, while the formula for volume or area cubed is

$$Length \times width \times height$$

That blue area out in front technically represents what the porch would look like if it was added. It's supposed to go in front of everything now because it's a receiving area for all the people and sacrifices that came into the temple. It's a flat area though, unless it's covered, which means we only have to find the floor area of the space. Our formula says it's length or 20 cubits times breadth or width. That would be roughly 10 cubits wide.

$$20$$

$$10$$

$$\overline{}$$

$$2$$

00

200

―――

200

Thus, the total area within the porch would be 200 cubits squared. Well, actually, the shape would be a rectangle since the sides don't exactly match. A true square shape would be exactly 20 cubits by 20 cubits while a rectangle would be something like 20 cubits by ten. It's called cubits squared though due to the area being found in the middle. In fact, can you pick out the square and the rectangle from the shapes down below? That's right, there's three in total with two rectangles present and one square. What is the square diagramed as down below? You got it. It says on it width. The two rectangles are called length and height as seen in the shape of the text.

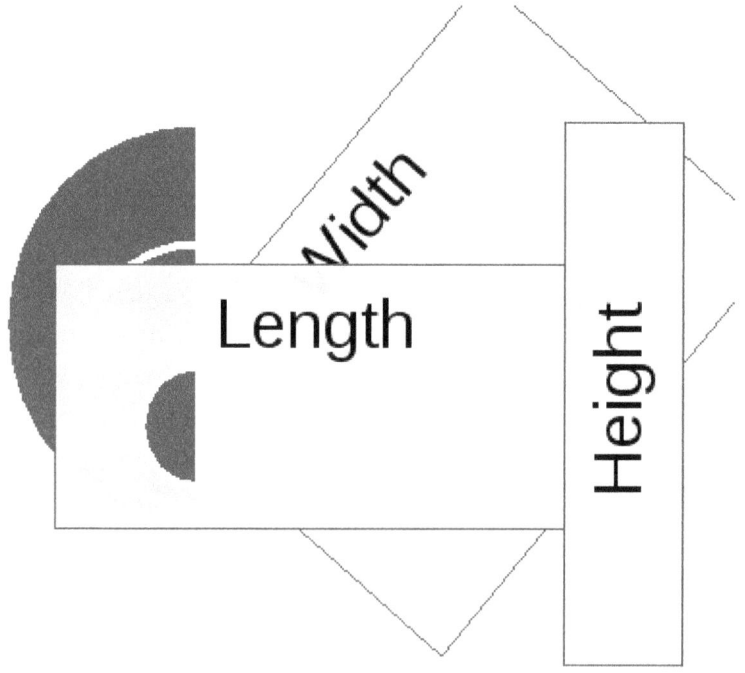

Then, what would the three blue things be called right there at the front? I don't think we've covered it yet, but they're known as semicircles. A semicircle is just a fancy way of saying a half circle. A whole one of the blue things would make a perfect circle. The circle always measures the same all the way around from that one point there in the middle. A circle that didn't would be known as an oval. Another way to tell would be to fold the circle in half and see if the edges meet. If they do, it's a circle. Then fold that in half one more time from the point in the middle just to be sure. If the edges don't meet, then you've found an oval from there. Remember the shapes of the orbits we looked at before? Most of them would be considered ovals while the planets themselves are usually a nice round circle in shape. The oval below is shaded blue while the circle finds itself a nice black in color.

5

6

Let's list it all again, just for a sum-up real quick.

Circle	• The same distance in all directions from the center • Measured in diameter from the central point in one direction to the edge
Oval	• Uses multiple points of diameter to describe • Often measured between the widest and smallest points from the center • Edges do not match up • It is not the same distance in all directions from the center
Square	• All sides measure the same length
Rectangle	• All sides do not measure the same length • Two opposite sides are exactly the same while the other two are different

Defining Space

And for the house he made windows of narrow lights.

5 *And against the wall of the house he built chambers round about, against the walls of the house round about, both of the temple and of the oracle: and he made chambers round about:*

6 *The nethermost chamber was five cubits broad, and the middle was six cubits broad, and the third was seven cubits broad: for without in the wall*

of the house he made narrowed rests round about, that the beams should not be fastened in the walls of the house.

1 Kings 6:4-6

Then from there, we've got something to discuss that appears on a building plot or a map. Actually, it's a special way of denoting the shape of a building that we call a blueprint. Basically, anything can go on a blueprint. It can look any way you like. Some people like to get all stodgy about the blueprints, their plans, and some lines. However, when it comes to the blueprint, or your plan for the building, the sky's the limit. You can do pretty much anything as long as it makes sense structurally and is well-supported with framing materials. Let's see if what he did make conserved any space. We have got ourselves three chambers or sitting areas inside, each with its' beams, separate framing, and rests. It already seems like an awful lot of space occupied just in building this thing already. Let's see if we're right.

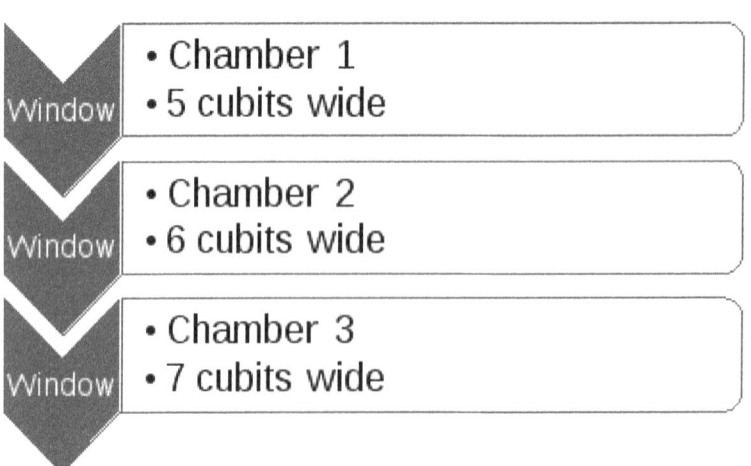

Who remembers what the total cubits were in the space of the floor? No one? That's what we're having building and design classes for, now isn't it. Technically, it's measurement but hush now. Don't let anyone know that this stuff has any sort of practical purpose. Let's make it all tedious, difficult, and rather hard to understand. Then let's see what all ends up. Then again, on the other hand, we could try making learning some fun. Let's put to it some purpose or such and see what comes of it, if anything much. Which of the two would you rather prefer? I think I'd rather something that's useful, don't you? What do you think of the design seen here in the text? All you really needed to know to answer that question was how long was the room. It was three-score cubits or 60 cubits in length, right? The sum of the three rests alone makes it take on a shape.

$$\begin{array}{r} 5 \\ 6 \\ 7 \\ \hline 18 \end{array}$$

There's 18 cubits taken up in the chambers or rests alone. That makes some 60 cubits minus 18 cubits left in the room.

$$\begin{array}{r} 60 \\ 18 \\ \hline 42 \end{array}$$

That's easy, there's 42 cubits left in the space. There ought to be plenty of room, right? Let's say, I told you the space was measured from outside the walls. Then what if you knew each wall was five to ten cubits in width. Wouldn't that information change the way that you think? All of a sudden, there's not so much space as it seems. I know one thing for sure, Solomon's temple was awfully crowded and dusty within. If you had thought that was grand, you'd have loved God's original design for his home among men. It was even made to be taken down and moved along with the people. How awesome is that to think that our God now walks among men?

Making Within

And he built the walls of the house within with boards of cedar, both the floor of the house, and the walls of the ceiling: and he covered them on the inside with wood, and covered the floor of the house with planks of fir.

16 And he built twenty cubits on the sides of the house, both the floor and the walls with boards of cedar: he even built them for it within, even for the oracle, even for the most holy place.

17 And the house, that is, the temple before it, was forty cubits long.

18 And the cedar of the house within was carved with knops and open flowers: all was cedar; there was no stone seen.

1 Kings 6:15-18

Speaking of space that has been lost, let's see what has happened now with the walls. Right now, I want to focus just on the measurements of all that has been made. After that, we'll discuss this issue separately of the different materials. Before we had discussed how much space was left in the house. The text here confirms our earlier guess. It was just as I feared. The house had been measured from outside the walls. Therefore, the space within is exactly 40 cubits wide. That's the available floor plan now. That means with there being four walls, each wall measures exactly 10 cubits in width. Therefore, the wall is 10 cubits thick from the inside to the space there outside. I figured that from what it says in the text. I just want to ask you this, before we've got some more figuring left to be done. When was the last time you've seen a 10-cubit thick wall? I know, I included a drawing for you to understand it much better.

12

Let's start with the figure above. The length would be 60 cubits outside. There's 40 some cubits left inside of the length.

$$60$$

$$40$$

$$\overline{}$$

$$20$$

There's 20 cubits spent in the walls, since that's what 60 minus 40 makes. Then, there's two walls, one on each side, that are part of the space. 2 walls into 20 cubits makes

2 into 20 (two goes in once into two)

(multiply two by one and subtract from the two)

$$2$$

$$\overline{}$$

0 0 (bring down the zero then on the other side)

(two isn't found in zero at all)

(let's add the zero to the right side of the one)

$$\overline{}$$

10 cubits are the sum of each wall. You can also double-check that by multiplying 2 by 10 if you want. The answer will be 20 cubits spent in the walls. Next, let's look at the little matter of why the walls are so thick. There's stone at their heart, with wood overlaying, and gold poured all over that. If you had the extra materials just laying around as Solomon did, it's always wise to invest in God's house. The only issue

though is these riches couldn't be withdrawn from it except in times of war and great danger. King Nebuchadnezzar did just that when he came up against the temple and melted the gold from the walls. After all, he had to feed the people he took. What better way to do this than by taking funds from God's house that Solomon built and deposited therein. I mean, if he had just stuck with stone he would've been fine. The issue is though that he'd just heard from the Lord, you see, about him walking after his ways for all of his days. Solomon, it seems, would take every bit of precaution he could just to hedge on that bet. He could trust in everything else, but not himself to do as he ought and so to follow God well. It's a good thing then, isn't it, that God had the people covered even when Solomon didn't. This second part of the temple was rebuilt in the time of Nehemiah only to be torn down shortly after Jesus came and died. Somehow though, the stones inside still survived. What a building, to be torn down time and again, yet it still ended up appearing at the strangest of times. This is what you refer to as what happens when you much prefer your own sort of way. The Lord's house had to be found of a different order then, that of his body, the true temple which came. It's on this corner then that the house, the frame, and all else now rests. Then again, how wide is ten cubits as we know it today? Let's multiply that by 18 inches per cubit and see what results.

$$10 \text{ cubits}$$

$$18 \text{ inches}$$

$$\overline{}$$

$$80$$

$$100$$

$$\overline{}$$

$$180$$

That makes 180 inches in width for each wall. Then, there's 12 inches per foot. To determine how many feet wide is that wall, we'll need to divide 12 into 180.

$$12 \text{ into } 180$$

$$12$$

$$\overline{}$$

$$60$$

$$60$$

$$\overline{}$$

$$0$$

The total ought to be 15 in feet. That's because 12 goes into 18 once. The total left after that is 60 because you brought down the zero. 12 goes into 60 a total of five times. Therefore, five is added to the right of the one. A 15-foot-wide wall is still pretty impressive to me. The maximum width I think I've ever seen a wall is perhaps a foot for very secure buildings and about six inches on average for building a house. Then again, no matter how wide or thick you're build your walls, our God is able to bring them down though they be ever so tall.

Bringing In

And the oracle he prepared in the house within, to set there the ark of the covenant of the LORD.

20 And the oracle in the forepart was twenty cubits in length, and twenty cubits in breadth, and twenty cubits in the height thereof: and he overlaid it with pure gold; and so covered the altar which was of cedar.

21 So Solomon overlaid the house within with pure gold: and he made a partition by the chains of gold before the oracle; and he overlaid it with gold.

22 And the whole house he overlaid with gold, until he had finished all the house: also the whole altar that was by the oracle he overlaid with gold.

1 Kings 6:19-22

Here's the very worst thing of all. The text makes it clear that this oracle made up the innermost holy of holies, where the priests would have gone to sacrifice before the altar of God. I suspect it was made of stone at first, though the text doesn't say. It's very likely, given the length, height, and width, that Solomon did this part just as he did everything else. The shape you're looking for though is a perfect cube that's, as the name suggests, quite tall indeed. In fact, it's 20 cubits times 20 cubits times 20 cubits all the way around. That's after all the other stuff has been added in though as at first. It's also designed to sit right at the front of the house. You'll see why I'm discussing this here in a bit. Calculate with me to see how wide this is in feet.

20 cubits

18 inches

_____

160

200

_____

360

So, we see, the cube is 360 inches in length, width, and height. Can someone say, God's good the whole year? That's how many days are in the year though, or at least that's what people say today. Maybe they're wrong though, who knows. If they are, how would you know much less find out? Perhaps the calendar of the stars might be able to tell us at first. What would happen if you totaled all the days up? There's roughly 365 in our modern-day calendar. What about the time of the ancients? Does it say or are there some gaps in understanding left in between? I don't understand how tall 360 inches is though. I could either do one of two things. I can take 12 inches and divide it into the 360 here or I could just multiply 15 feet times two. If you paid attention, this is roughly double the sum of the thing we discussed just before.

15

2

―――

30

At last, you've got a wall that totals 30 feet high. This is starting to sound rather uncomfortable like something else that we know. If you can figure what that is, please avoid shouting answers out. It goes back to what we discussed before with Solomon's temple being a symbol of before the rebellion fell and all there.

Making Arrangements

So Hiram gave Solomon cedar trees and fir trees according to all his desire.

11 And Solomon gave Hiram twenty thousand measures of wheat for food to his household, and twenty measures of pure oil: thus gave Solomon to Hiram year by year.

12 And the LORD gave Solomon wisdom, as he promised him: and there was peace between Hiram and Solomon; and they two made a league together.

1 Kings 5:10-12

It looks like we've finally come across the payment for all the building that had been going on. You may or may not know this for now, but when you do a lot of building as Solomon did, you'll need to do one of two things. The materials and people to do the work are needed as at first. Unless, of course, you have people doing it of their own free will. That certainly is not the case here. Solomon was just blessed enough to get it all done. Let's look at how much it cost and how exactly he did so. The materials are easy, it seems, with their being free. Well, technically, they aren't really for free. These required payment of food and oil to be given in exchange for cedar and fir. I mean, if you think about it, these natural resources were likely all that country of Hiram's had. They needed some food so it seemed. Solomon could easily make off on the good side with this in exchange for some yearly support. That way, since he didn't have everything Hiram did, he pretty soon would. They'd do what's called a trade, you see, so everyone soon would be filled. Imagine being without something which you really wanted or needed to make you happy. Solomon had houses to live in aplenty. One thing though he lacked was what with all to build his father's dream, a house for the Lord. Then on the other hand, Hiram was hungry you see. Economically speaking, it meant a good deal. Let's look at the apparent value of the cedar and fir in addition to a lifetime of friendship and support gained in this trade. It was worth approximately 20,000 measures of wheat and 20 measures of oil in perpetuity to be given as long as he lived. Let's say one measure of wheat cost five dollars in these days and times. That would be 20,000 times 5.

20,000

5

―――――

100,000

Don't forget to put all your zeros in place there. There's four of them counting from right to left with the addition of the one there on the end of the ten. That would be 100,000 dollars which is a lot of money in this currency. Let's try to convert to another currency besides the dollar. Suppose one dollar equals 100 in another currency tokens. Let's make up a name for it and give it a value. I'll call it the byte. Sure, that's another name for computer data storage, but let's forget about that just for a moment and see what ends up. I'll need to multiply 100,000 dollars by another 100 in the newly minted byte.

100,000

100

―――――

000,000

0,000,000

10,000,000

10,000,000

That would be wheat worth 10,000,000 bytes to you. I'm just gonna get a bunch of investors to back this really quick, if you don't mind. That'll make my new byte value real. Can you see that this is not a very good way to do markets or anything else? Sooner or later, everything will run out of value and probably funds to back it all up. Then, we're gonna do just the opposite with the oil. Let's say the oil is worth more in that day which is why he gave less. It's gonna be oh, I don't know, about 10 dollars in value. There are 20 measures of oil which needs to be multiplied by 10 dollars to see how much Solomon paid.

20 measures

10 dollars

00

200

200

There you have it, a nice round sum of 200 dollars a year in oil. Let's try converting the dollars to Hiram's economy. The sum of choice in that day was probably just that, a measure which is what gave it the name. It's like saying I'd like a cup of something today. It doesn't matter what it is I'm asking for as long as the cup stays the same. However, if it's flour I'll get more and if it's oil, there'll be less. Although technically speaking it's all the same since it's filling the same size of cup. If all we knew was the 200 dollar value and the 10 dollars exchange rate to make a measure, we'd divide 10 into 200 to come out with a 20.

Hiring of Men

And king Solomon raised a levy out of all Israel; and the levy was thirty thousand men.

14 And he sent them to Lebanon, ten thousand a month by courses: a month they were in Lebanon, and two months at home: and Adoniram was over the levy

1 Kings 5:13-14

Solomon has to have some way to get all this work done. His best way to do this is to hire all those who aren't busy with harvest or defense. To do this, he'd have to figure out who wasn't busy with what. Back in that day, there was no better way to do that than by what we know as draft. They called it a levy though just to be clear. It was sort of like a mandatory showing reminding everyone of the work to be done. Then too, he had to hire them. To do this, he likely sent out messengers to bring them all in. The other way to do this was to wait till a feast day when all were gathered there at the temple. There was 30,000 hired in total, though not all at once. Let's say everyone got a dollar a day for wage. That would be 1 dollar times 30,000 to make exactly 30,000 needed to hire them in sum. He gave them this over the course of three months though. There was only 10,000 men sent out each time around. We'll divide 10,000 into 30,000 to find out how much he spent on a monthly basis. It goes in three times, right? Therefore, he sent out 10,000 in labor expenses each month. Wait a minute though. That's just 10,000 for one day of the month. Each month as we know it today lasts about 30 days. We'll have to multiply 10,000 times 30 to find out the sum for that month. Then, just subtract 4 days of rest from the sum. That's either 10,000 dollars times 4 days which makes 40,000 dollars off the sum or 30 days minus 4 times the result. Let's try the one at the last: 30 minus 4.

$$\begin{array}{r}30\\4\\\hline 26\end{array}$$

Then multiply 26 days times 10,000 to make the result.

$$\begin{array}{r}10{,}000\\26\\\hline 60{,}000\\200{,}000\\\hline 260{,}000\end{array}$$

260,000 dollars a month is quite a lot for these times. If they had worked all 30 days without stopping for the Sabbath, it would've made a total of 300,000 to be paid. It's quite a lot for all things considered much, really.

Locations

Perspective Shifts

Back in those days though, Solomon's workers would've been paid out in coin. At least, they were in the times of our Lord. It's much the same principle see. Back in those times though, it would've been paid out in coin likely only enough for each man to be affording of food, shelters, and clothes. Then again, how much was each man paid in those times? Let's say each coin equaled a day's wage almost. It only makes sense for all these to be paid out as such. Don't you see how the inflation that large amounted things like the dollar produces can prove to be harmful of course? Transferring this back into coins actually produces a much better sort of approach. That way the economy doesn't look like it's perpetually on the brink of disaster that happens naturally as large numbers of these are first introduced. In much smaller funds, it's only the sum of about 260,000 coins. While still quite a sum, it isn't as large or as threatening at first. Considering too that it takes about 100 much smaller coins known as the penny to make up a dollar, I'd say you've got the better end of the times.

Back a few years ago, everything was much more reasonably priced and perhaps based off the smaller coins that made up the larger units from which the dollar consisted. Obviously, not to be teaching economy lessons, but your own currency will vary greatly in its estimation or value attached to these different types of amounts. Let's say you could have all your smallest economy values known as the money together in a pile on the right. Do you know what the names are for these values and how much each token engenders? By the term engenders, I don't mean whether it's male or female. Coins aren't in the habit of taking on physical gender or form. Rather, they have a set denominator or common amount in between them of course. For instance, in my currency, it's a penny which is the smallest amount of the dollar. It's written something like this $0.01 and I'll need 100 of them to come up with this $1.00. The much larger category, the dollar gets put over here on the left. It doesn't make sense in terms of, to borrow a cultural expression, dollars and cents. We've also got on the right-hand side the dimes and nickels down too.

If you don't know what the equivalent is in your currency, it's perfectly fine. I'd just rather you found that out first before attempting much of everything else. The dimes can be expressed as a $0.10 or ten cents of a dollar. It takes exactly ten of these bad boys to make up a dollar or ten pennies to make up a dime. There's the nickel in waiting over here too. It'll look like $0.05 once it's written. Five pennies go into a larger one of these and you'll find two of them in a ten or a dime. Given that ten dimes make a dollar, you'll need twice as many or twenty nickels to get the same type of result. There's one more piece though that's been in the waiting. It's the quarter or $0.25 cent piece proper. Two dimes and a nickel can equal it's sum along with twenty-five same total pennies. Since it's expressed as a fraction or ¼, you'll find exactly four of these come out to a whole one of these $1.00. Back in the good old days, so they say, these tokens were used for something besides just spare change. You could've actually grabbed a whole handful of them and gone shopping. Granted, it might not have bought a whole lot, but it would've been enough for one or two meals. Wages also were paid out in similar sorts with good money being made for just a few of these tokens. You might be over here wondering what's happened. That's corporate greed for you and also some pride. What happened was those big men in business just decided that wasn't enough. That's when prices rose and wages along with them before everything sort of just fell. You'll see a similar result told of back in the days of the Lord. There's a table where I've expressed the result and also added some space for you to write down your own currency small coins and also some figures.

Coin	Today's Sum	Actual Value
Penny	$0.01	
Nickel	$0.05	
Dime	$0.05	
Quarter	$0.25	

Your Currency	Today's Sum	Actual Value

For the kingdom of heaven is like unto a man that is an householder, which went out early in the morning to hire labourers into his vineyard.

2 And when he had agreed with the labourers for a penny a day, he sent them into his vineyard.

And when they came that were hired about the eleventh hour, they received every man a penny.

10 But when the first came, they supposed that they should have received more; and they likewise received every man a penny.

11 And when they had received it, they murmured against the goodman of the house,

12 Saying, These last have wrought but one hour, and thou hast made them equal unto us, which have borne the burden and heat of the day.

But he answered one of them, and said, Friend, I do thee no wrong: didst not thou agree with me for a penny?

14 Take that thine is, and go thy way: I will give unto this last, even as unto thee.

15 Is it not lawful for me to do what I will with mine own? Is thine eye evil, because I am good?

Matthew 20:1-2, 9-15

Actual Value

And they sent out unto him their disciples with the Herodians, saying Master, we know that thou art true, and teachest the way of God in truth, neither carest thou for any man: for thou regardest not the person of men.

17 Tell us therefore, what thinkest thou? Is it lawful to give tribute unto Caesar, or not?

18 But Jesus perceived their wickedness, and said, Why tempt ye me, ye hypocrites?

19 Shew me the tribute money. And they brought unto him a penny.

Matthew 22:16-19

When addressing much smaller sums such as these, the discussion never fails to turn up a few other unrelated sorts of the issues. We're talking about actual value here for a second, not about what you'd ideally like it to be or even which opinions society engenders. Once more, there's that little word engender again. It's almost like a what's next on the agenda, only this time it's being used to express what's remaining from the much larger collection. Let's say as of today a penny will get you exactly one snack if even that. Ideally, you'd need about one hundred of them in some more modern thrift shop locations to get only one thing but of course. Back in that day though when Jesus was teaching, the penny had an unknown mutual value. I know, the times they sure are a-changing and along with them the markets. Just think of what a penny could buy in a few other places. Let's say I go to a culture where one dollar equals round about 800 tokens. If you don't know it just yet, a quick search should reveal your local exchange prices. We'll call your unit of currency though a token for lack of a more exact form. It could be rials, lakhs, or even a shekel. Here's how to express that in just about any account.

1 dollar: 800 tokens

That's the proper way of expressing what's become known as exchange. Basically, you're trading one unit for another which really is a whole lot of nothing. I'll express it as a penny at first, which should be written something like this.

1 dollar: 100 pennies

Because

1 penny: 0.01 dollar: ? Pennies: 1 dollar

Let's try to figure out the ? pennies on from there. Watch what I'm doing closely at first. We'll have more opportunities for trying it later.

1 penny x 1 dollar = 1 |

0.01 dollar x ? Pennies = 0.01?

1 = 0.01?

Next, divide the 0.01 into 1 on the other side of the equation to get

100 pennies solved in for ?

I take it doesn't answer your questions any better than this? Thankfully, most exchange platforms at this time are fully automated and all this isn't actually needed. Let's say, you're going down from one dollar into the culture. That's what it'd look like at first. Only, I want to know how many pennies you'd have for 800 tokens in a dollar. We'll express it like this.

1 dollar: 800 tokens: 0.01 dollar: ? tokens

1 dollar x ? tokens = 1? |

800 tokens x 0.01 dollar = 8.00

1? | 8.00

1 divided by 8 = 8

? = 8 tokens

You'll find that 800 tokens go an awful long way on from there. Except that it doesn't really, and you know why that'd most likely be? That's because the markets are all linked together through international trade or exchanged up at the top. Its how money gets passed around from one place to the next. The circulation usually stays in places of power like a few centralized countries while leaving the poorer ones well out of the loop. Let's say you don't have very much to bring to the market. There are a couple different ways of getting the funds. You could say trade or move funds from one place to the next. Sooner or later, one place will be entirely emptied and bare without anything that's been left for the taking. Think though, that's only if there's not funds moving back in return. If the funds only moved in one certain direction, which so often happens in charity cases, it'd make the second place absolutely dependent on stuff from the first. Ideally, in this case, you'll want to take some time investing around in localized markets or in the developing of something that matters. You'll want to send goods or service in exchange for the first. Just maybe though you'd willingly be accepting of help with the promise of some growth upward much later. A truly fair and equal market between forces like countries would have each one bringing the same amount of stuff to the table. The exchange rates would be roughly equal without huge disparities occurring between them. Basically, all that's a fancy way of describing something as unfair as it seems. That's where you'd get terms like first, second and third-world from when referring to countries. They're really not making no sense though at the first. In the text, we see the Pharisees' disciples along with those supportive of Herod, a local leader, have come forth in crowds. They brought the penny with them to ask a specific opinion, though it's really not meaning of much. I mean, I can't find the penny addressed anywhere else. We'll look have a look at some of the other currencies later. I fear there's some though a good bit much older. The penny then has come to be the lowest common unit of value, which may or may not have been very much in those days. We're not entirely sure on the details just yet.

Individual Basis

20 And he saith unto them, Whose is this image and superscription?

21 They say unto him, Caesar's. Then saith he unto them, Render therefore unto Caesar the things which are Caesar's: and unto God the things that are God's.

Matthew 22:20-21

It seems here's the actual sum of a penny back then just as it is in our times. The thing is really that the penny was much more than just a glorified goodwill token. Instead, it had as many so often do an individual's face there on the coin. It's much more of a shifting in focus to think of this image actually being Caesar's of course. I'm sure the design of the penny might've changed with the times, but not in its name nor hardly even the game. Pretty wonderful that such a thing has gone on down through the ages. Remember too how that had looked once before all that had happened. Caesar was once a pretty powerful man of that time ruling all the way from Rome, which technically speaking was an isle from way over on the opposite side of the sea. It was connected to land so it wasn't much of an island there really. Rather, it's a place from which Rome conquered and grew. Ruling in those times came by military right rather than destiny. That's to say fortune had indeed favored the brave at such a time before as it gave. In fact, the Roman empires of Jesus' time and possibly later was vast, stretching all across whatever worlds had been known. A penny would've been considered tribute as fitting as this to bring to a king. Consider, he was little more than a military general in his own rights who once worked for his wage. Now though, the people are doing some for him by bringing him these. Well really, they weren't brought but rather sent at request. The better question would've technically been how many of these were required for what sorts of villages, for how many, and at which certain few times of the year. Then, men such as Matthew would've been involved in the set-up, collection, and passage of stuff. The issue at hand though isn't whether paying taxes was needful. Rather, you're be a lot better to wonder that a penny was all that's required for a day of upkeep as Jesus had said. Think of it without such a pointed muttering down deep in your breath. It was all money could buy of that day, that much and more. We've gone over the needs once that much already. I'm not in the habit of repeating things over again to be sure. It was something this Caesar would've done well to remember. To a man paying taxes though, it would've been hardship for certain to go about obtaining such for the food. Though, had all men paid taxes, it would've formed a never-ending cycle of upkeep for the few. That's to say the little were made into many and so became much.

Bartered Sum

And the people saw them departing, and many knew him, and ran afoot thither out of all cities, and outwent them, and came together unto him.

34 And Jesus, when he came out, saw much people, and was moved with compassion toward them, because they were as sheep not having a shepherd: and he began to teach them many things.

35 And when the day was no far spent, his disciples came unto him, and said, This is a desert place, and now the time is far passed:

36 Send them away, that they may go into the country round about, and into the villages, and buy themselves bread: for they have nothing to eat.

37 He answered and said unto them, Give ye them to eat. And they say unto him, Shall we go and buy two hundred pennyworth of bread, and give them to eat?

38 He saith unto them, How many loaves have ye? Go and see. And when they knew, they say, Five, and two fishes.

Mark 6:33-38

Let's talk about what'd happen if you didn't have any pennies, lucky charms, or even a few goodwill tokens. There's how to get them of course, usually through work or begging from off the blessings of somebody else. There's very few who'll actually go about giving out large sums for nothing it seems. Back in Jesus day, it wasn't for nothing but rather for the comfort and companionship gained from the people. Think of it as he went around mostly with nothing to give though at all times needed unlike some of the few. Not that I'm saying there weren't some that needed a little more time, care, and attention. A prime example of this was the beggar which met Peter and John going into the temple.

He asked them for money when just a healing was all that would do for fixing the problem and solving the evil. Had he only been given money time and again, well, there weren't any doubts really. The vicious cycle of want and need would've only continued for certain. Saving him perhaps in the form of a healing was the best thing that could've possibly happened. Consider what then of the large crowds which seemingly came out of nowhere as though drawn to the Lord. Some have said it was only for food but I think they've followed him for whatever else he could offer. Just think of it as large crowds came out of nowhere in the most desert locations. We'll see more of it later for sure. The word on the street least as far as the text actually goes is that they'd known him afar off even that of the Lord. Funny thing too, the Lord felt obligated to feed them somewhat whenever appealed.

That's the best part of the whole thing in the bargain is the very decided lack of all this. You know, the provisions and stuff of whatever was needed at times such as these. First thing you'd think of when meeting large crowds of people was how much their absence from work and all that sore would be missed not whether they could all spread out again to go inhabit the towns. Clearly, these are some more unnatural creatures or beings or people not ones that should probably thus have gone off from their homes. Certainly, I'm not saying that any should rise from the dead in this fashion much less what they'll look like should these thus then appear. So, to avoid all the guesswork and such, let's just stick with what we already know as them that are merely in need of the Lord. He's not going to just let them go hungry, now is he? Rather, he'll feed them and teach them and given them a reason for staying around him much later. After he's done surely, they'll go on back to their towns. The point though I'm making isn't what's been done but now just about how it will happen. Thus, you might wonder how you're to go about feeding all these new hungry hundreds of people. Jesus and his disciples were able to make enough of a living from the occasional harvest of crops, returns back to their boats by the sea, and whatever gathered there the people could spare. Here though, it's something of the opposite sort of an issue. Food for so many involved, first of all, a supply or else some money to buy it with as the disciples had said.

Think of it sort of like this. If you can't afford to buy with coin as at first, you can always do a trade or a barter for stuff. To do that though, you've got to have something of roughly similar or equal in value to make it all worth your while. Over the years people have bartered with work, wares, or whatever's needful most at the time. Two-hundred pennyworth of bread in that day would've been fit for a king. Certainly, it would've required a taxing to get it for sure, cause it's hardly likely that a bunch of guys going down to catch fish from out of the sea would likely have very much either. If you remember, the fish that was for dinner instead coughed up a coin for the repayment of taxing much later. With funds like this, Jesus could've had something the envy of Caesar himself if he wanted. Small wonder then that the disciples were always constantly asking about his soon returning the kingdom back to the people. Though it really wasn't about the funding or lack thereof when really the followings what mattered as unto the Lord. That's assuming first off though that anywhere around was large enough to actually have such a store. Remember, the former recommendation from disciple headquarters itself there for the taking. Supposing there wasn't enough to go around then in plenty, regardless of how much actual money, the people were better off dispersing back to their own homes and towns. Regardless, we'll see the Lord handling the matter again in a bit.

Insufficiency

When Jesus then lifted up his eyes, and saw a great company come unto him, he saith unto Phillip, Whence shall we buy bread, that these may eat?

6 And this he said to prove him: for he himself knew what he would do.

7. Phillip answered him, Two hundred pennyworth of bread is not sufficient for them that every one of them may take a little.

8 One of his disciples, Andrew, Simon Peter's brother, saith unto him,

9 There is a lad here, which hath five barley loaves, and two small fishes: but what are they among so many.

John 6:5-9

Well, looks like the trouble comes in when you finally determined just how large the sum following him actually is. As usual, whether for the first time or many more after, Jesus just had to go on and feed them again. I mean how could he not really when his heart towards them was nothing but care for the people. Whether it was mercy, pity, or whatever, regardless, he felt for the crowds. Funny thing is really, I think there was a bit of his human side too where hunger came in. That means at times he felt as though he too had the same types of needs. Therefore, his caring was sort of more of a 'let's eat' rather than a pity me snack. That being said, the crowds were so large and food was so scarce that 200 penny-worth wouldn't have fed a whole unit. Sure, you could've fed them with bread, the cheapest thing to be had that was visible. Though really, if you wanted a much closer comparison, it wouldn't have bought all that much fish or loaves with it either. Just think of the little boy who brought his whole lunch of five loaves and two fishes in to the Lord. Let's say it might've been gotten for say two pennies or twenty. It all depends on the market though and how expensive these are really. Let's say that you could've gotten five loaves for a penny by chance. Do you know how many could had with say 200 pennies and change? Real quick now cause I'm not planning on extending the classes. It's right about 1,000 loaves just fresh for the taking which isn't enough say if you'd passed around mouthfuls. Jesus though didn't half hardly do it by halves.

Instead, he had plenty in store and just a little bit more. The fish could've been caught in the wild or just thrown off on the side in the bargain. Though seriously, all things considered the prices of goods really does matter. When you've got things priced super-cheap like this around a whole lot of people, you're bound to be making enough for a killing. In all honesty though, a killing's what will be had if there's not enough work that's needed or givers or takers or earners of coin. What's to be done then in times like these you wonder. In the perfect world, we'd have everybody go in all day say for a penny. Though in the much more perfect world of the Lord, the same work would've produced the same wage whether for all day long in the heat or just a few hours then at the least. He'd have everyone make a fair wage that's more than enough and fit for a king that you'd see. Then at the least, everyone would've had roughly the same amount of coin to spend. Supposing it was only as required to make a decent day's living, it would ensure they'd never run out with a constant supply. Though that's all things considered if you're say willing and able in making a living. Next time, we'll find out what'd happen if the penny wasn't the smallest unit of sum moving around in the land.

Tribute Fund

And he spake unto Ephron in the audience of the people of the land, saying, But if thou wilt give it, I pray thee, hear me: I will give thee money for the field; take it of me, and I will bury my dead there.

14 And Ephron answered Abraham, saying unto him,

15 My lord, hearken unto me: the land is worth four hundred shekels of silver; what is that betwixt me and thee? bury therefore thy dead.

16 And Abraham hearkened unto Ephron; and Abraham weighed to Ephron the silver, which he had named in the audience of the sons of Heth, four hundred shekels of silver, current money with the merchant.

Genesis 23:13-16

It all started way back when with the shekel being the standard unit of measure moving around then. It seems that Abraham here had just lost some of his family members, kin, servants, close relatives, or friends to old age or whatever thing lurked unforeseen through their midst. I don't know about you but I'm also new to that time, not having been around, when shekels were first introduced. Back then, people tended to go a bit crazy around money, especially when foreigners and strangers it seemed. Well, they still do to this day just the same sort of way. Think of how the stock markets have all gone a bit crazy and everything that can be gets inflated really. Basically, it's just a fancy way of saying they jack up the prices from there. Certainly not because it's wanted or needed or industry standard of course. Rather it's done for want of a better term the lack of a fold. I don't know about you but four hundred shekels for a piece of land in the deal all seems rather much. Here Abraham got himself gyped in the bargain. Not to mention the loss of his own kin made him all the more anxious to grieve. Thus, he would've settled for whatever Ephron suggested. Far cry really from when he paid out to

Abimelech only seven things of the fold. I'd quite forgotten if they were sheep or some oxen. Either way though, Abimelech was more than happy to see them if you'll remember. Sure, Ephron could've had other reasons such as times of war or disaster when it was actually needed. Still though, we're not quite sure how much a shekel is though not quite this sum. Sure, Abraham could've easily gotten it through minting or trading. I mean, after the Lord blessed him and his rescue of Lot from going after the kings, it seems he only made his way up in the world. Then again, he would've had a lot of possessions. enough to travel with ease wherever he pleased. Along with him were herdsmen and flocks, though it's not quite clear if these were paid or else had a living with what's termed as a wage. Basically, that would've meant that their food and shelter was covered along with everything else actually needed. Since money wasn't considered a need when your living was already paid, Abraham could've just held on to the profits from there. One more thing you'll need to know about this matter of funds. The shekel has remained till this day though not quite possessing its original value. What that was, we're not too sure from the start. Perhaps it'll tell us as we go on much later.

Numbered Shekels

This they shall give, every one that passeth among them that are numbered, half a shekel after the shekel of the sanctuary: (a shekel is twenty gerahs:) an half shekel shall be the offering of the LORD.

Exodus 30:13

Well, the numbering of the shekel among other coins really is something, isn't it? Now I'm not sure how much a gerah is. Nor does Scripture ever tell us. Let me tell you though, if you can find it, let me know and I don't mean with the other odd denarius or silver pieces floating about in the midst. I don't care whose image or inscription it is unlike the penny. With that one, it'll always be about a penny and most probably with Caesar himself trotting not too far on behind. I'll be the most surprised of all though if you can find some basis for equal measures of this. Look in Scripture though, not in some man's old printed book where the pages get dry and crumble with the ever-present passage of years and nothing ever changes if at all ever not with stroke of writer's pen or the sudden movements say of the Lord. That's to say, it's best to make sure your books, unlike your currency, have some room to breathe and to grow. If they don't, something, somewhere is dreadfully, terribly wrong. It's mostly because his book is supposed to be filled with his Spirit with life in his Word. So too, does it swell and grow with every few passage of years. If your currency does that though, it'll be a bit more pressing sort of an issue that we'll see very much later. Basically, a shekel, as the text has said, is twenty gerahs. I sure couldn't tell you what a gerah is, but you could think of it as the smallest measure almost like a penny is of these times. Half of it though, or ten gerah at first, is sufficient to make offering to the Lord. This money will be used for the upkeep of the temple as well as needs of food and some hunger and also shelter of all of the people. Regardless, having a collection done for religious reasons sounds like a pretty good notion. At least, it does for saving up much later and perhaps also investment of sorts. Then again, having all these huge crowds and large groups of people, really has done much for spreading the wealth thinly between them. As seen just prior, it seems Abraham has likely no issue with four hundred shekels laying round doing nothing of course. Now though the wealth has spread going down through the people. Through trade and whatever else between them, it's enough for all to have say a little. It's not very much though at the time, just enough to make a decent sort of living and have enough for sharing between them. That is, if they can afford their own household, they'll also go in for having a shekel. That's cause mainly census struck them at first which is an accounting not of the Lord as you and I probably heard.

Upkeep of Money

Also we made ordinances for us, to charge ourselves yearly with the third part of a shekel for the service of the house of our God;

33 For the shewbread, and for the continual meat offering, and for the continual burnt offering, of the sabbaths, of the new moons, for the set feasts, and for the holy things, and for the sin offerings to make an atonement for Israel, and for all the work of the house of our God.

Nehemiah 10:32-33

It's now the time of the Babylonian captivity. Nehemiah was a prophet who documented the people's return, efforts at rebuilding the city, and their temple much later. Basically, you could say, it's what makes the culture special I guess. Well not all that special really. Consider this, after all the years of Babylonian upkeep and rule, the shekel still retained its original value. You could say it was more than common being found in the land. Everyone used it then and later probably preserved for all posterity for commonality reasons. That's because the coin's value was silver sufficient for weight and also some change. The only thing though changing was the people's estimations far after. Let's say the Pharisees paid Judas thirty pieces in exchange for a life. An offering required then would've only been half a shekel much later. It's not that weights attached to it had changed very much either. Rather, the value or price put on that life was different I guess. You could've said that Jesus had much more potential than most of that time. Thus, that's the driving force behind the offering thirty at first for face actual value. The only thing that changed though was the people's attention I guess. Leastways, work during Babylonian days would've been few and far between even with the enemy that roamed through the land. Well, times would show much later with the "remember me my God for some good" that such always wasn't the case. You'll notice first off, that whatever wages these had would've been saved up as unto the Lord. In this case, the fund was at 1/3 or one-third of a shekel only. The other two-thirds would've been kept back for themselves or else used for whatever was most definitely needed. That's to say, they would've ended up putting it back then to work. What's going on with the other one-third that used much later in making the people? Sure, some had need of food and shelter as seen once before.

Governing

Troubles in Cost

And I bought the field of Hanameel my uncle's son, that was in Anathoth, and weighed him the money, even seventeen shekels of silver.

Jeremiah 32:9

And thy meat which thou shalt eat shall be by weight, twenty shekels a day: from time to time shalt thou eat it.

Ezekiel 4:10

Is it just me or has the land lowered in costs? With all the people spread out through the land, it's highly doubtful the land values hadn't risen very much really. Far cry then from Abraham's four hundred shekel purchase once before and the seventeen shekels of Jeremiah and his nephew later. Similar realty to be sure, each overlooking a field though not where these were originally planted. Purposes though shouldn't matter when it comes to the buying or selling of land. Let's just say time has a way of evening the balances allowing stuff to happen. Not because all that's a bad thing, really. Just know that from Abraham's time on down, there has been a decided over-valuation of land. Now it's all come to a halt. By Jeremiah's time when the nation has begun to go captive or missing, the cost of the land has all but lost in its value.

Instead, people are placing the value elsewhere on what's much more important. Can you think what's more important than money but the sustainment of life? Should anyone tell you otherwise, well, they're just faking it really. Trust me, the preservation of life and everything needful is foremost in place. That's made more than abundantly clear when the sum of meat to be eaten in siege totaled in weight to twenty-some shekels. Basically, the Lord's telling the people to make themselves matter. Say it with me now: there's food, shelter, and everything else. We call this instead of a de-valuation, a returning to total sum profit where the nephew's been idealized along with the land and some coin to return. We call this, instead of a de-valuation, a returning to total sum profit where the nephew's been valued along with the land and some coin to go with it. There are those people in today's day and age who like to criticize that the value of money is tanking and society with it. All that's just a theory of course when compared with the rest of the book. You'll soon see that justice follows this returning to sense.

Balancing Acts

Ye shall have just balances, and a just ephah, and a just bath.

11 The ephah and the bath shall be of one measure, that the bath may contain the tenth part of an homer, and the ephah the tenth part of an homer: the measure thereof shall be after the homer.

12 And the shekel shall be twenty gerahs: twenty shekels, five and twenty shekels, fifteen shekels, shall be your maneh.

Ezekiel 45:10-12

It seems by Ezekiel, there's been distributive justice brought back to the land. Let's see, the shekel ought to be fixed firmly at twenty gerahs as a lesser form of the change. Probably smaller, say, than the penny that'll come after. Then again, all the weights should be fixed firmly in place and not visible to the slow, inevitable creep with the times. That's because there's those who wish to make profit off these, that of the ever-present human condition. Seems there's not much to do for the issue besides letting the Lord take the lead on it, really. Before we go, here's a figure of all things considered. Regardless, knowing and fixing the points of what it's worth is key to keeping the markets all sort of balanced. That's also how you can fix point the market and so correct it by righting exchange. From there, the price of the goods and distribution around in the people can follow.

Coin	Today's Sum	Actual Value
Gerah	Currently unavailable except for archeological value	20 of these make for a shekel
Shekel	$0.27 of a dollar	½ tax collection 1/3 upkeep fund for temple 17 for land in captivity 30 for Jesus 20 for meat by weight for daily consumption
Maneh (also spelled mina today)	$0.65 of a dollar	20, 25,15 shekels likely dependent on material Can also refer to 30 pieces of silver

Different Perspective

Hear this, O ye that swallow up the needy, even to make the poor of the land to fail,

5 Saying, When will the new moon be gone, that we may sell corn? and the sabbath, that we may set forth wheat, making the ephah small, and the shekel

great, and falsifying the balances by deceit?

That we may buy the poor for silver, and the needy for a pair of shoes; yea, and sell the refuse of the wheat?

Amos 8:4-6

As we'll see later on, having huge inequities, better known as things that aren't fair, isn't really good for the soul. Even so there's having huge economic disparities roaming around through the land. Last time we'd addressed the various notions of sorts that enabled this thinking. It was a perspective of too little, not enough, just right, and a little too much. I'm not saying we'd be soon paid a visit by Goldilocks and the three little bears, but you know if the shoe fits why not just wear it I guess. Then again, Goldilocks herself had an issue before the end of the tale. I mean, who wouldn't with three bears of various sizes that had all made a nest in the human-sized beds. Poor Goldilocks, the human child, all alone and in desperate need of a second opinion of sorts. Perhaps the sage voice of wisdom quite would've helped her back then. Remember, the story's told how too little, too much, and just right invaded her house and ate just about everything there was to be hard there in sight. By the time they'd finished, poor Goldilocks had just had enough and it wasn't too much.

We can't blame her for feeling this way, can you at first? Let's say though some had by deceit or some other crooked sort of measures conspired together either for gain or some profit. I can well imagine their frustration of waiting to sell again in the land. That doesn't excuse though their actions much later. Let's say they'd decided to fix prices by increasing them which would've also raised their margins for profit much later. You know, when you're selling grains and some wheat, you can either do one of two things. You can either send them out to an outside supplier of you can decide to do something quite besides all that. Doing so will distribute and sell and manage your profits abroad in the land. Let's say though this middle option is dishonest of sorts. These sellers could falsify records, keep the profits all for themselves, or fail to inform the bringers of such all for say a pair of good shoes.

The other thing that happens though is when it's something you've labored for or quite possibly have grown. You could start feeling a bit too entitled, just like the men who'd worked for a penny at first, only to find themselves overcome by the burden and heat of the day. Never mind the fact the penny was still quite a sizeable sum. Perhaps it was more than a shekel or less. It's really hard to tell as at first. Though when you think of it really, the shekel and the other values are based off their weight and the currency backing them, which is the face value of coin. Caesar's coin, the penny was backed by his image. Though common, it was valued entirely by the rest of the people. The shekel though, made from the silver, was based off the weight and the silver prices too for what it's worth as the basest of metals. This too remained fixed, year after year, to prevent ravages like Goldilocks' house from keeping occurring. Perhaps you'd call it having company over, whoever knows. Regardless though, it's wrong of a sort and the result is the same but of course. The poor and the needy are left utterly destitute and their own house besides after the three bears have already left. It's how it starts off with the little things that make up the rest. In times like these, the Lord is despised and the rest too of the sort.

These here can't wait for the times of religion and customs to be gone from the fold since the only thing left to them is the money and not their own sort of people. It's what happens though when there's other things prized that money can't buy. Let's just say the health, fellowship, and everything else ought to be top-care from there. We're past the time of the three little bears. Then again, there's another sort of opinion that's what happens when the measures and prices fluctuate later. Either it can be done through an open market opinion as the price of one runs up all the rest of the fold while measures get scarcer and scarcer. The other thing that could've been was not allowing all this to have happened. Sure, it takes some foresight and sneakiness with an unloaded if not more accurate form of a measure. Then again, you'd have to have eyes on the skies, basically everywhere that's a market-place really. That's where business licenses, like some places have, happens to help. That way, it's everyone's problem.

Then again, too much regulation can greatly hamper the poor of the land of a sort. That's where selling the poor for silver and the needy for shoes comes from then at least. It's like saying that really, people aren't worth all that much. There are times when these too can't afford the license and fees that come with registration and all other if those main regulations. A better way of doing it then is by installing balances where the transaction happens, so to speak. On the whole, fixing the currency at a set rate where manipulating the economy won't really happen. Then again, they're selling the last of the crops as scrap then for food. It's not really fit at that point for consumption by humans or other creatures who'd happen to boast. At this point, you'll have to install a valuing of human life later that's more than just profits engendered. Once more, there's those strange little words. It means in short, the profits obtained through this strange sort of a means. Next time, we'll look at how a valuing of life just happens to help.

Values of Life

But he answered one of them, and said, Friend, I do thee no wrong: didst not thou agree with me for a penny?

14 Take that thine is, and go thy way: I will give unto this last, even as unto thee.

15 Is it not lawful for me to do what I will with mine own? Is thine eye evil, because I am good?

Matthew 20:1-2, 9-15

Well, that's sure where justice comes in at, just before the life after next. Last time we saw the justice being wrought in the land. It finally had gained a more fixed price in value based off the land and not just the results. I mean, really, you needn't explain to anyone just what you're doing yet, do you? Then again, an explanation sure would've helped make it more visible. I'm going somewhere with it all, just bear with me though everything seems all run away with for the moment. Just after, we just saw how fixing the markets wrought more justice in the local economy sector. From there, we've got another matter of fixing the wages. If not, these things are liable to get all out of sorts. I know we've seen it before but a prime example of this is the laborers sent abroad in the vineyard. Well, the text didn't say really, though I'd always assumed it was laborers brought forth to the vineyards. That ought to be a lesson for how dangerous assumptions are for starting opinions. Let's say, they could've been working anywhere for a penny. The point of the matter though wasn't the length of the day nor the heat endured along the way.

In these days and times, it's become years and experience worked if you happen to think of it really. It's all just a matter as simple as replacing the words. The way of fixing this then so the coin is fair to everyone and equally distributed is paying the same amount to everyone regardless of hours worked or actual labor. After all, a living wage is alive so it seems. I'd settle for just enough for a family therewith, but we'll see more on that later. After all, struggling all day for the living is scarcely worth the life that you're given. Thus, let's say there's only a set amount of coin to be had therewith. Not making a whole bunch more, unlike the workers, solves this problem though perhaps the issue is not how much coin is produced but rather the size. By paying everyone the same sort of amount, you'll ensure that all is fair and equally distributed to large numbers of people.

Technically, you could've had a lot more come in for all different shifts in varying times and amounts but the numbers of pennies would've all mattered. You can wonder how that would be while the hundred or so laborers standing around in the market aren't there for free. Technically, the owner was hiring whomever he found there at first, which meant with wages like that, the men wouldn't have had to go back to work for a while. It might've been more than a day to be sure, depending on family size and what their intent was to happen. Though, I don't recommend saving up for very much later since you're better off trusting in God to provide for the rest. I don't see what the harm is in a little prior planning of sorts for sure but of course. In fact, that's why we're here really.

Justice Restored

And I heard a voice in the midst of the four beasts say, A measure of wheat for a penny, and three measures of barley for a penny; and see thou hurt not the oil and the wine.

Revelation 6:6

The issue here is that the penny looks like it's finally lost all its' former value from there. You've probably never heard of de-valuation before. Basically, the value is how much worth is put on something by how we esteem it. In Christ, when he was esteemed smitten by men and afflicted, we saw him as nothing more than a suffering Savior or a had been martyred figure. All that depends on your viewpoint of course between how you see him and how you know him as later. It's gone on back to the same value of a person that we'd from the start. We'd like to say that we all value people quite highly and also their time but do we really. As this whole discussion on the economic sector shows, perhaps there's some justice involved that needs to come forth from the Lord. Even if it doesn't begin first at home, you know, there's some place to start. What's the best thing that can happen then to the market besides each one getting valued for their person and their own useless opinion. As justice is brought through the land of restoring the markets from one place and into the next out, it appears this way in a number of forms.

The way the land prices appear fallen off all by themselves with no interest based on the land or its value. Then again, speaking of justice, it so happens that the original owners thereof should have something of sorts then to say.

That's a notion of ancestral ownership and shared interests in common much later through the Levitical law which allowed it to happen. There's this thing we just saw, where Jeremiah could redeem the land of his family for what it's worth based off its value. Basically, it was a pay off the debt attached to the land but of course and also a clear-off their name. It's an idea that seems strange to those in the west at first from the start. In parts of the world though where individual interest gets lost to the tribe, the tribal individuality gets valued very much really. I mean why wouldn't it, technically speaking, when it's tribal lands on which these had lived for many hundreds of thousand years. Basically, the fathers' fathers had the run of the land and so too their sons. Alright, so when you've got a bunch of other new people coming on in, you'd have to be accepted by much of the tribe. If it's a family house, the same goes for the family of course.

It goes without saying, really because you can't have environmental justice without a regard for the local laws and customs that have been from the start. That's part of the reason why land prices to Abraham were so high as at first when the local identity had got itself twisted. If you think about it, the same things apply in the markets. The second way value gets shown to the person is through lowered prices attached to everything needed like clothes and food and also some shoes. That's not to say the makers of this are suffering, really how could they, when there's the third possible attachment of value hidden in sight. Can you guess what comes next? That's right, it's matters of the same types of the wages. It not only saves money but rotates through a whole bunch of people for whatever hours and times that they're willing to work for whatever's most needful. The only time where this system breaks down though is on introduction of skilled manual labor. These are tasks where some training is required to finish. Still though, that's no reason for it to be the same year after year with each one being called a slave of the system. Then here's the fourth type of valuation attached to the person and that is the family proper. No, you don't think so? It's all come on back to where order reigned as at first. I'm not sure how much a measure is except that it's really supposed to be fixed. This prevents what you'd call an inaccurate system of measures where the scrap of the crop has been passed off as a whole but in fact. Here though, it's quite the opposite same sort of a system. You'll get three measures of barley for a penny or so and also some wheats.

Basically, it's enough to bake a whole kit and kaboodle, that is to say a family, some buns in the oven, or some loaves in a pan. Then, there's the oil and the wine to be had in the bargain, kind of as a garnish than an afterthought later. If that's not value being packed into the penny, I don't know what you'd call it then if not whole disaster of sorts. Certainly, the days of picking and choosing between one and the next would've long since been over it seems. Then, everyone would be selling in plenty, though perhaps making the same as the workers of course. It'd be a break-even right in the middle or enough to keep the whole thing going right on from there. With prices and wage fixed like this, there's actually more money floating around to each of the sellers due to more people being able to afford the priceage of wares. Then again, it's not very nice, is it to just have assumed.

Assumptions in Fact

Judge not, that ye be not judged.

2 For with what judgment ye judge, ye shall be judged: and with what measure ye mete, it shall be measured to you again.

Matthew 7:1-2

That's why it's not nice to have assumed things at first due to their strange and unnatural proportions. Mostly, it's what you blew it up into really, your opinion that is and the matter that's just been affected. Alright, let's get right down to business from there. You'll remember, we were just finishing our little discussion of what had gone missing from the rest of the world. Well, it's not really gone missing has it but rather taken or quite gone, for lack of a better term, mad then about it. Here Jesus has just got done with going on about the value of people and creatures and how these have all mattered very much then to him. The perspective or viewpoint it seems all ties in with the rest. How, you may wonder? Basically, all that's to say that not everything seen is perfectly visible. Judging without knowing the rest of the story, or in this case the full facts of the matter, is only the root cause of the issue. Had you only but know that the whole economy issue seen in the hiring of Solomon's men would've run nearly throughout the whole rest of the country.

I mean, how could you have really when everyone else was last seen leaving in droves. That's back then though. We're talking about now and the heart of it from the start. That's about like having judgement without any ministry. Let's say we decided on what we're eating just fine. I'm sure you couldn't tell me what we're discussing, could you? Ah yes, we're at judgement just for the sake of having an argument. Better yet, we don't agree with anyone else so let's just find something to dismantle right quick. Let's say too you don't like my own personal style regarding the matter. We could say the same things about each of us no matter on which side of the coin you're standing or the isle for that matter. There are reasons for that, you see, and they lie within the guides that go with the letter. You know, the spirit of the law and the guides to go with it to match. When you're talking about law and the justice that follows, you're dealing with much more personal matters. Much like a man, the law also exists in three separate parts. They're all different at first, apart from the other, but without which they wouldn't be whole from the start. Real quick then just in case you forgot.

Judge not that ye be not judged

That's the body matter really. It tells me what and what not to do with my mouth and anything else in and around the whole judgmentive process. Let's say that can involve arresting someone and locking them up. Some societies have the notion that reforming the culture works best through padlock and key. Only, they've bolted all the doors and windows shut and quite thrown away the key now that you see. At least, there's none around here to be found. Maybe if you tried looking anywhere else it'd be visible and then I wouldn't have to go on judging again. It happened so much, it's become a bad habit, really, almost like something I've gotten used to quite from the start. Then we'll see what there'll be after that.

For with what judgment ye judge

Ye shall be judged

This refers to in short the content of the law or its sum. It's what comes pouring out in the behavior with the body considered. You can tell anyone you please to put up, sit down, and hush that much for sure. Though without regulation, this part is like what'd be forming the soul. There's not too much you can do about this part right here aside from a sit down and feed it some spiritual lessons, some long hard struggles, or battles to fight but of course. They say time's the best predictor of learning but you can't educate it or explain it away as simply as that.

With what measure ye mete it shall be measured to you again.

That's known as the spirit behind it. It's what lets you think and sense things in other dimensions beside just the one that we're currently in. Really, it'll all make a lot more sense to you in a moment from there. A measure basically is the way in which we're dealing things out. Let's say you didn't like the way in which I was chasing the issue around through all of our classes. We'd both agreed there's an issue for sure. I, on the other hand, have a bit better point of a view on it perhaps than you. Maybe I don't though and that's where the whole judging part has just returned from the start. Looking back, I can see now that what Solomon did wasn't necessarily right but also not really a wrong. Did it make sense for the times? Of course, it didn't really find issue back then that's one thing for certain. What about when applied to this time that we're in? That's where it starts to find issues from the judgementive proper. As we already see, should I start applying dollars and sense, well Solomon's economy is in for some issues. It doesn't quite make sense from there and that's where we'll start finding some issues. Speaking of this, we'll also have problems again in a minute when it comes these all those at work in matters of judgement. Surely there's got to be a better example than this, maybe one that's applied to our markets and business and all things considered.

Jumping Jehoshophat

> *3 And why beholdest thou the mote that is in thy brother's eye, but considerest not the beam that is in thine own eye?*
>
> *4 Or how wilt thou say to thy brother, Let me pull out the mote out of thine eye; and, behold, a beam is in thine own eye?*
>
> *Matthew 7:3-4*

Try something with me now if you will. If you won't, well, I'd rather wish that you would have again.

> the centurion's servant or the nobleman's son

Nobody's laughing yet? Why not, whatever has happened? Let's keep it going of course. Sum sounds an awful lot like a son at first does it not.

> the terrible steward or the widow's last mite

Then becomes

> the unforgiven debtor of course mixed in with the prodigal back home with the Father

and we're there once again. I can keep on guessing around if you like, though I'm sure you're not much in the habit of remembering these stories as visually told. Jesus would but of course, because they're of his own back at home. Speaking of which, that's the

> king leaving his throne just in time for the banquet much later

because the story's not stopping then not for nothing just yet till it's all been, happened, and then.

The servants though were angry along with much of the men

Which became

the guests standing in for the wedding as though nothing had happened. One in particular though was missing his clothes which somehow ties in with the missing lost lamb, and the oil which ran away from the lamps and everything that's lost in the house being found once again. Though it's not entirely said over and done yet is it then? You've still got to stand and answer the Lord about what's become of his clothes.

Yeah, no, I'm sorry I haven't a clue as to what just happened. I'm the last person who should be saying any of this I guess cause it's not my place once before. It's his though and that's what ultimately matters. How's that for being appropriately planted and then? I take it's not a question easily answered which is why

the Lord will have a few last minutes to work it all out feverishly in a flurry of counting and sorting.

Somebody send help then I guess, oh, but just wait. He already did once before, from there and back again, just in the distance that it takes from one nail scarred hand to the next. Perhaps some water would desperately help with the dryness that's been found in the text, though, I doubt very much really it would actually help. See, the problem

as with Lazarus all hung up and dried is his not coming forth from the tomb with the single last one little breath of the Lord.

Society

Sequentially Speaking

Better sit yourself down and hold on tight at least for a while until all is completed. Be patient though with the process because it takes some time for all to be worked out from the first. Well, worked itself out isn't quite the same as having someone else doing the working out for you, now it it? It's sort of like saying everything's been taken care of when it hasn't been really. Unless, of course, you've gotten possessed with that sneaking little suspicion that it hasn't, not in the slightest or at the least, if you want to get technical about it really. There are only two gemstones left to be found along with a large amount of other precious metals which aren't as they seem in getting mined, or in this case refined, from the earth. Lest you'd think John was a visionary or otherwise crazy, there's a few others just like him from Peter to Paul that are also supporting this view. We'll see more about the theory of heat in the undoing of bonds as it blends together with substances and breaks all the molds.

First though, it's come to my attention that Jacinth is pretty high up there in electrical levels. Remember, those pesky little electrons moving in orbits that we looked at before. The chemical composition for Jacinth which is the next stone in the sequence, can be written like this $ZrSiO4$ which means zirconium base mixed with silicone and oxygen later. I'd say it's oxidized all the way through for that one no matter whether zirconium or also the silicone when it comes to mixing it all very well and fully together. You'll notice the table below for your closer inspection. No need to memorize it yet because it won't be needed again. You'll see why in a minute, as we go through the theories of space and matter all smooshed in together without time in the bargain relatively speaking.

Just know though, that's elements fifteen to one hundred that we've found to be mostly so far that are working.

The other stray 58 to 71 and 90 to 118 are all either not commonly used, except in nuclear reactives from there, or aren't a part of the most commonly used everyday applications. I mean, it sounds pretty silly to put it that way really, when elements 1 to 14 are all most highly prized in space, mechanical, and engineering settings. Then again, you didn't hear me say this but all the gemstones make pretty good rockets once set off from pressurized settings. That's why you'll want to use safety when attempting to make these much later and not to say put them in your nearest local pressure cooker and then seal off the lid. That is unless you're into canning and stuff. Pressure cookers make wonderful things for achieving that perfect vacuum tight seal that preservatives love and also mason jars in case you were wondering. Which I know you weren't, really, I just thought you'd appreciate the helpful sort of opinion.

Element	Electron	Proton	Neutron	Levels
Phosphorus				
Sulfur				
Chlorine				
Argon				
Potassium				
Calcium				
Scandium				
Titanium				
Vanadium				
Chromium				
Manganese				
Iron				
Cobalt				
Nickel				
Copper				
Zinc				
Gallium				
Germanium				
Arsenic				
Selenium				
Bromine				
Krypton				

That's not zirconium yet, is it? It sure feels like it should be in there somewhere. Maybe in a few other tables we'll find it very much surely. It sounds almost like naming off students, doesn't it, one by one at a time. It'd really simplify matters a lot, couldn't it, if we lumped class all together and just took them outdoors. I mean, why can't you, since like students they've all got needs and levels and grades. Thinking of it this way makes everything simpler and why shouldn't it really? It's not like you've got to memorize them all, just be familiar with them if they should appear again later. Think of it now just for a second. We'd seen the leap between sulfur and chlorine before, hadn't we? No? What about between salt or sodium and the sulfur just by adding in water? Is there even an element sodium? It feels like there should be one in here somewhere at least.

Element   Electron Proton Neutron Levels

Rubidium

Strontium

Yttrium

Zirconium

Niobium

Molybdenum

Technetium

Ruthenium

Rhodium

Palladium

Silver

Cadmium

Indium

Tin

Antimony

Tellurium

Iodine

Xenon

Caesium

Barium

Lanthanum

Hafnium

Come to think of it, I haven't seen gold run through here just yet. I've seen plenty of the other metals though such as tin, silver, copper, nickel, and iron which is strange considering gold is technically one of them too. Then we've got the gases like xenon, argon, bromine, and chlorine but there's no oxygen in there either. It really should, shouldn't it be in there too? What about water for life? It's a substance found in abundance and very much required for the sustaining of things. In fact, if you boil the water you'll find your oxygen vapor. That's why bromine isn't really a gas, much like the oxygen, but it probably should be cause when you've added in heat that's what you'll get in plenty amounts. We haven't found the zirconium yet, have we? You got it, it's halfway down in the table right up above. Whew. That's still not all the elements yet, there's still a lot more though to go.

Element Electron Proton Neutron Levels

Tantalum

Tungsten

Rhenium

Osmium

Iridium

Platinum

Gold

Mercury

Thallium

Lead

Bismuth

Polonium

Astatine

Radon

Francium

Radium

Actinium

We've done all that work and I'm tired already. I think taking a break sounds like an excellent idea, don't you? If you don't feel like one yet you very soon will. There's one more thing wrong with the table that I'd like you to find. Do you know what it's going to happen to be? Those of you who've been paying attention to health will already know it just yet. That's right, it's the salt or the sodium which hasn't come in with the rest of the elements proper. I'd have listed them out for you all nice and neat just so but now you'll know there's a few main types of uses according to where each is found in the earth but of course. There's earth, metal, mineral, air, and the few others found in the body besides just that one resident poison. Can you guess what that is? You got it, arsenic, right from the start. Then too the elementary table has all but forgotten about the oil on which it depends or the gas essential for all civilized life. How's that for some forgotten about classes, a few ideological notions, and some half-baked ideas. If I didn't know better I'd almost certainly concluded that they're hiding the least little thing useful. Here's the rest of the listings though of the elements just so you know I'm not forgetting or God forbid making stuff up that we'd like to have happen.

Rutherfordium Bohrium   Darmstadtium
Cerium   Promethium   Gadolinium
Thorium   Neptunium   Curium
Dubnium   Hassium   Roentgenium
Praseodymium   Samarium   Terbium
Protactinium   Plutonium   Berkelium
Seaborgium   Meitnerium   Copernicium
Neodymium   Eeuropium   Dysaprosium
Uranium   Americium   Californium
Nihonium   Flerovium   Moscovium
Holmium   Erbium   Thulium
Einsteinium   Fermium   Mendelevium
Livermorium   Nobelium   Lutetium
Ytterbium   Tennessine   Lawrencium
Oganesson

> There you go, I found what we're after. That's Sid the Sloth from our very best friend that I've only just let back in again. Don't worry, he's quite harmless really. The real enemy is what he's just been running from out there in the cold.

Something that Matters

Even so we, when we were children, were in bondage under the elements of the world:

Galatians 4:3

I don't know if you've only just noticed, but there's something going on with the elements around here, something that everyone's missed. Well, it's not just here but everywhere too, isn't it? I couldn't have hardly been the only one to find that something's a little bit off besides just Sid the Sloth. You'll have to excuse him at first cause he's from a different period of time than this. It's one that was very much borne from the cold. It chilled your bones and so everything froze. I don't know much about the legions of men. Perhaps some like the Eskimos that live in ice houses called igloos with fur round their nose are just made for the cold. You know, they've got those little things called parkas, made from animal skins. Perhaps it's survivable with the right sort of equipment, all other things considered. Just maybe though, it's what's left of the cold back when everything froze.

This was back in Paul's day back when Christ came here and died so you know there's some truth to those words really and maybe even soon some hope and life in them too beyond just what we knew. It sounds pretty at first if you don't know what you knew that our God never grows tired or lonely and so never gets old. Even so though, haven't you ever wondered at all the accounts and stories that told of it thus. There's somewhere in Siberia and a few other places that haven't thawed round the globe, that stay perpetually cold, with some creatures trapped still in the ice it is told. I don't know about you, but that's a bondage for sure. In fact, there's a few that've said the permafrost layer in some places hasn't thawed to this day. That's that part of the earth, you know the layer that lies up above deep down under the first. With all the heat way down under the earth's surface down at its core, there's a fire that stays perpetually cold. You'll see it erupting in volcanoes in some places as up from the surface. Mostly these are Sub-Saharan deserts or some lonely tropical islands. However, there's outliers with this as all things included would tell.

For instance, the volcano in northwestern America lies dangerously close to the permafrost's position. You can also wonder what's wrong I suppose as there's freezing and burning simultaneously occurring round in the globe. The two just don't sound natural in the same sort of a sentence. Nor does the opposite position of those that agree with what was termed as the ice age once proper also propagating that the earth is continually warming. Well, which is it then, because I didn't think both are occurring at once. It sounds like a bondage of sorts if you'd asked me for sure. You know, with what all the freezing and burning of earth all at once. Perhaps it's gotten somewhat tired of these sorts of conditions as well, you can't be too certain.

Elemental Confusion

But now, after that ye have known God, or rather are known of God, how turn ye again to the weak and beggarly elements, whereunto ye desire again to be in bondage?

Galatians 4:9

According to modern dating technologies, which really aren't anything much aside from ascribing the earth to hundreds of millions if not billions of years, the ice age occurred in roughly the 1600s and lasted for about three centuries or more. That's because modern dating technologies using things like radio carbon become inaccurate or invalidated with the age of decay. That's because depending on how quickly the body was buried and in what substance ensures the speed of decomposition. It's something that police departments in some places haven't caught onto yet and the tv shows are way ahead of their times. Nevertheless, it's an explanation that makes sense really in terms of half-lives and all the stuff of that sort. Basically, the half-life is the fullness of a life that hasn't been lived to its fullest potential as of just yet. It's kind of hard to though when you're dead, fossilized, or just plain frozen in large blocks of ice for a tomb. Thus, in all things, there's some part of life however faint that lives and breathes and longs to take shape once again.

The longer it's gone, the fainter these chances become which is where scientists come around with their fancy-pants methods. In terms of probability of this life living again though once it's been buried or frozen is one in a million or so, which makes sense looking at the dating's in terms of decay. Though when you've got God on your side those chances are never at zero but always at one. I'm willing to take it that all the scientists running around haven't yet met up with the Lord. This means quite simply that the ice age, while still technically a really cold period of time in the earth, has been going around in some places for a lot longer than originally made out from the start. Peter here referred to this elementary rebellion in, oh I don't know, about the first century or so as reckoning from the time of Christ's birth. There's a very good chance it was going on in Paul's day and Peter's much later and also in John's case as well which is when he saw it all tumbled and fell.

Let me tell you, it's awful hard to love your own wife or respond to your husband when you've technically been frozen. I know, you're not believing any of it just yet much less swallowing it whole as we go. Think of it though. Let's real quick run through the facts once again. Remember those listings of elements that I rattled off at the last? They all had one thing in common and that was famous people or places, or even last names. I saw a Tennessee in there and America too and even a few of France and Liverpool, England and one of Moscow in Russia. Then come in the ones that are bearing their names. There's Einstein and Curie and Rutherford and Mendelev to name just a few. Ytterbium too is a cogitation of yttrium from a few tables back earlier. It sounds very much like somebody's been tinkering with the elements to make them to serve, sort of like a modern-day slavery to speak of much later. Then I looked at the functions of the elements seen round the table. The amount of metals beyond just being in electronics and buildings and processing are too many to count besides being core to some of the meds.

I know, you don't believe it just yet. Many of them are labeled for use with chemotherapy which is a modern-day treatment for cancer and the rebellion of cells. In case you'd wondered, the cells in your body start growing super-fast all at once. It can start off with one certain tissue or focus and then spread to the rest if not corrected at first. To treat that rebellion, science and medicine have figured out how to give you combinations of metals and vitamins fed through IV. That's an intravenous line for those that were wondering though some of them take the form of powders and pills. They'll make your body really sick too while they're correcting the issue. It's sort of like sending in heavy artillery to an area, isn't it, when all there's been is unrest. It makes sense to give them some good hot food, warm blankets, a place in to rest, and to send them to bed. Come to think of it your body cells in this manner sound just like that decay that seeks life from the first.

It's a bondage for sure to be in a position as this. We call it by some other names though just for show. Then too, have you ever wondered why at 32 degrees Fahrenheit, or whatever the equivalent in Celsius just happens to be, we don't all just freeze. Everything else is for sure from the water that's been laying around to the snow on the ground. Your body composition too is about 80 percent water or so then. That means you're rightfully 80 percent frozen when the temp drops below zero. With blankets and layers, you'll have a couple days of life like this if given shelter and even some food though just a house made from snow. Which is more than water left out in barrels can boast of as that too starts just to freeze. There are a few elements on the table too that make up your food. They're stuff like iron, calcium, potassium, manganese, selenium, and perhaps a bit more. Though sodium isn't on there, as it should be, nor is the water which is why in winter they've taken to salting and sanding everywhere that people will go. It makes sense really cause it's the only thing keeping water from turning to ice on the roads. Come to think, it's sort of like what Jesus said of the salt that had lost its savor and was good only for being thrown out and trod underfoot of the men.

If there was really say an elemental rebellion, only the salt then is faithful. It's this thing in your body that keeps it from turning to snow or more frankly into dust once again later in the say, bone-chillingly cold. Then there's the last thing that makes the conclusion. It's that thing of the discovery of elements in only the 1700s at the hands of the French. Before that, these were known quite simply as precious stones and some metals or as elementals to the alchemists just prior. Science then had got half hardly sort of invented but the alchemists already understood more than that even through their poisons and art from the start. It was they that had developed the idea of bringing things from one state and into the next using what they already had available at their ready disposal. They also had tried turning rocks into gold without quite as much success I am told. These left their thumbprint on the table as seen in the sudden appearance of arsenic there with what was once considered a poisoner's cure. In fact, it's what clued me in on what had just happened. Still though, it doesn't solve the one last final issue of the elemental rebellion and what's to be done with it really if anything much.

Jacinth

Remember how we'd talked about the chemical formulation from which Jacinth was made. In case you forgot, it's ZrSiO4 cause too much looking up isn't good for the soul. At least, not when such small things are considered as these. Turns out the largest places to find zirconium is in small coastal waters. The coast though reeks of the sea and its salt waters contained within it as well. These are at rather warmer to cool temperatures judging from whence it's usually mined. The sands found under the waters below are just full of this mineral. It's also partly a metal though due to its properties in between the equation and such. Basically, you'll want to have seawater that starts off cool just at first then warms to a nice temperature that feels good to the touch. It won't be too hot, just warm enough. Then the sand needs to settle down at the bottom. From this, the zirconium is formed. Zircon is another precious gemstone though of lesser apparel. Zircon is usually occurring when the waters have cooled where the sands have solidified into a bunch that then appear as a stone. A little polishing though soon cleans these things up. A little potassium though I'm told helps in the process. I'd try it both ways and see what results. It might be a lot more than expected. Anyhow, you'll want to then treat the sand that's just been refined with a thorough mixing of oxygen and hydrochloric acid over relative heat.

Hydrochloric acid is basically just salt that's been refined by the heat either through a mixing with ammonia or by just distilling the base. Make sure you've got the solution in a sealed off container though and then add in the water. Better yet, just add in the water right off the bat and stir in the salt which will then boil out into the air as a gas and then condense from the steam. That way, you'll always have plenty of liquid that's there and ready for starters. Though you'll not want to drink it because it's strong enough to burn through your clothes. Then, add that to the sand-like zirconium deposits and stir in magnesium over relatively high heat in a large pot. After all that's done, it'll resume a somewhat metallic appearance that some have suggested needs purification much later. In this case, given that jacinth also occurs in nature, I'd say wait till the end of the process to see what results. Naturally occurring, it's found in hot desert sands or perhaps some places where water had flowed. Then on top of that, you'll add in regular sand. Mix it all over moderate to high heat just like without allowing the metal to cool. From there, be sure to add in plenty of air for the oxidizing process with stirring, blenders, and such. There, how's that for a pretty red stone just fit for the making.

And thus I saw the horses in the vision, and them that sat on them, having breastplates of fire, and of jacinth, and brimstone: and the heads of the horses were as the heads of lions; and out of their mouths issued fire and smoke and brimstone.

Revelation 9:17

Amethyst

Let it be known quite simply that the chemical structure for amethyst is $SiO2$ relatively speaking. It's found mainly in desert areas or those that are prone to have floods. Also, it's known from its origination in pockets of active volcanos. Perhaps some had long since gone inactive when they're doing the mining of stone. Regardless, amethyst comes in many sizes, types, and colors which range from clear to reddish and purple. Basically, it comes from the crystalline structure of quartz which is clear like unto glass that is blown. Here in these cavities though, the sand mixes with earth which has traces of iron in it instead. Without the iron inclusion in much smaller amounts than would otherwise matter, the amethyst might even be some other color. As the sand is heated and gets molten under the volcano at first, you'll also notice it mixing in with water as well that's got turned into steam.

This then is what promotes the two-fold mixing action along with secondary oxygen inclusion. That alone will be enough molecularly speaking for the breaking of bonds. If the mixture when heated is bubbling much, that's all well, good, and fine since you'll want that which creates the blips and ridge of the stone. It'll have one solid core down at the middle with much larger stone formations around just like a flower. Don't forget though not to stir it at all as it's left then alone. The lack of stirring action won't be enough to preclude oxygen mixing, though the bubbling action probably will more to be sure. By far, it's probably the easiest stone to make though hard on the patience as known then to time and creation.

Waiting for Later

But the day of the Lord will come as a thief in the night; in the which the heavens shall pass away with a great noise, and the elements shall melt with fervent heat, the earth also and the works that are therein shall be burned up.

Seeing then that all these things shall be dissolved, what manner of persons ought ye to be in all holy conversation and godliness,

Looking for and hasting unto the coming of the day of the God, wherein the heavens being on fire shall be dissolved, and the elements shall melt with fervent heat?

Nevertheless we, according to his promise, look for new heavens and a new earth, wherein dwelleth righteousness.

2 Peter 3:10-13

That sounds almost amazing from there, an unlooked-for day of the Lord, does it not. The issue though is hardly the day. More than likely though it describes a time period in general although a day to be told can be sure. You know how Peter had said that a day with the Lord was as a thousand years thereabouts or so on from that then. Come to think of it really, you'd need about that much time to appreciate fully the depth of the issue. The elements though are what we're focusing on right at the moment from their state at the first. It seems these had rebelled, been taken captive, or otherwise misused throughout the ages of man. It's just a story though really some background for appreciating fully just where we'll end up in just a few moments from here. Basically, the heavens and earth passing away is hardly anything new we're already told. John confirms it in Revelation as we'll see much later or so on and then. Nor is that hardly the end of the issue. There'll be a new heaven and a new earth taking their place but not before the old have fled away from their place in the light of his own glorious face. Though I'm hardly not trying to claim the Lord's glory for myself or so also his place.

You'll just have to trust him from there I suppose cause that's where the story conquers and grows. The text confirms you'll have a great noise like the kind that's made from the atoms being dissolved therewith or cast then asunder. It can also come from your 'oooohhhhssss' and 'aaaaahhhhssss' whenever anything happens the least bit out of its place. Let's say there's some smoke and some burning at first. We all know the works will be tried by fire as at first, whether they be gold, silver, wood, hay or stubble just to ensure that everything is on Christ the chief cornerstone laid. I don't know about you but there's tremendous power found in molecular bonds and things of that nature. Say if that power stored up were ever released, it would be as with all things a treat at the least and more than that. Cause the last time atoms were being released for their thunder, it toppled whole cities and legions of men from just a little thing as small as, well, I'm not really sure.

Turns out I haven't seen one before and neither should you. Due to the atoms so small of a size and their nature, studying them takes place in highly specialized vacuum pressure environments that are tightly controlled, locked down, and sealed with a lid against accidental explosion. Again, it's due to the nature these erstwhile things bring with all others remotely considered. Anyhow, it's a pent-up energy to be sure, probably nothing short of a miracle. Consider if all these were controlled by some highly specialized upper level elements of the same nature, the names of which were recorded for posterity later but at least at the moment so you'd know who's up and running the show. Then again, a rebellion would make some awfully sick since nearly everything we live in or use even down to the ground that we walk on and the breath in our lungs is made up of these I suppose.

It's called radiation sickness and symptoms range from mild to severe later on depending on how much and in what amounts you were exposed. Which coincidentally, is pretty much what happens whenever someone with cancer has taken their chemo. This is what science has termed a therapy of sorts or some sort of cure. Though when has curing a poison with poison in additional shapes, sizes, sorts, and a nature ever been as effective as those. That is to say, fighting fire with fire seldom results in water rushing forth from the sort. In fact, it's madness to think anything of that nature could be much less to happen. The last time radiation sickness was recorded on any appreciable level came right around the discovery of some of the upper level elements of that type and nature. You'll have to look harder than that to find any sort of connection yet there's one out here hiding in the open at least. I take it you've never wondered why there isn't some sort of combustion reaction taking place whenever you touch something from which atoms take up most of the space?

For all this logic, there ought to be loud explosion taking place in almost constant locations. That is to say it'd be nearly everywhere at once. The sound I'd think really would be deafening to say the least. That's because I'm afraid the lower level elements encountered most frequently are more stable in nature and reactions from these. As you go further up in the table or number of all things considered, the elements get less and less stable to the breaking of bonds. If you're thinking in terms of nuclear fission, this is technically what releases the energy stored up on the whole. Then too, melting this down will result in lower state levels with higher stabilities than previously mentioned. This stability is especially important considering the many countless supplemental metals that have to be added in order to keep a structural integrity system.

You know, when you're building materials you have to have alloys or combinations of two or more metals to make things half as strong as they should be very much really. Funny thing is some of the hardest things in the world are just made out of sand. Therefore, you could say that while the silica has the highest stability out of all the upper level stuff and some figures, it's also not really prone to reactions. Therefore, that's where the fervent heat comes in spoken of in the text once again. Come to think of it, technology flickers, burnouts, slowdowns, and errors are all part of this fervent heat that accompanies the Lord and his just. While I don't know which form the new heavens and earth will come in for sure, there won't be none of the old bondage left to the first. Nor will there be a very much fallen in nature that kept these things from serving and doing his will as seen in their continual harassment of God and his people. Think of it a bit like this as I'm currently writing with technology glitches.

Thank the Lord for his provision at least cause otherwise I'd be starting all over from beginning again. I mean, from the first-wards part of the book till the end. I'm not sure if this technology slowdown just has issues with the Lord and his Word or if it's just something else that somebody has thought of just yet. How's that though for a fervent heat of a sort of should I looked for a response much greater than any previously mentioned. Though the application of heat at least is really important for maintaining stability and keeping a good sort of relations. With the advent of all sorts of things that were previously unheard or in an unlooked-for way sort of later, you'll want to maintain the walk of the just. Just in case you know, Heaven forbid, there's some rather sentient feelings. From there though, with the Lord on your side, you should be very much fine I suppose. Until the new creation then thereby is founded, I'll trust you in peace to leave with him later.